P9-DDW-099

ELECTRICITY
AND
MAGNETS

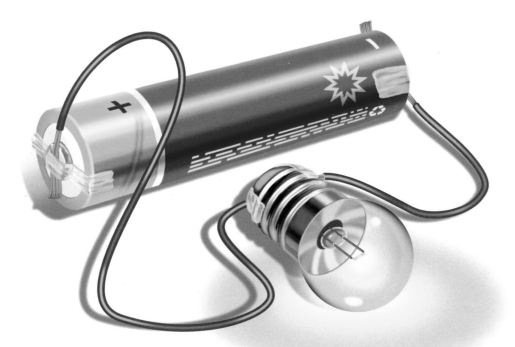

Sarah Angliss

KINGFISHER
NEW YORK

KINGFISHER
LONDON & NEW YORK

Copyright © Kingfisher 2013
Published in the United States by Kingfisher,
175 Fifth Ave., New York, NY 10010
Kingfisher is an imprint of Macmillan Children's Books, London.
All rights reserved.

Distributed in the U.S. and Canada by Macmillan, 175 Fifth Ave.,
New York, NY 10010

Created for Kingfisher by The Book Makers Ltd.
Illustrations: Peter Bull Art Studio

Library of Congress Cataloging-in-Publication data has been applied for.

ISBN: 978-0-7534-6784-8

Kingfisher books are available for special promotions and premiums. For
details contact: Special Markets Department, Macmillan, 175 Fifth Ave.,
New York, NY 10010.

For more information, please visit www.kingfisherbooks.com

Printed in China
9 8 7 6 5 4 3 2 1
1TR/1212/UG/WKT/140MA

Note to readers:
The website addresses listed in this book are correct at the time
of going to print. However, due to the ever-changing nature of
the Internet, website addresses and content can change. Websites
can contain links that are unsuitable for children. The publisher
cannot be held responsible for changes in website addresses or
content, or for information obtained through a third party. We
strongly advise that Internet searches be supervised by an adult.

Contents

Getting started

Every time we turn on a light or watch TV, we are using electricity. When we close the fridge door or answer the phone, we use magnetism. If you've ever wanted to know what electricity and magnetism are, how they work, and how we use them, then this is the book for you. It is packed with activities and things to make. Before you start, read these pages carefully—they give you a lot of advice. A few minutes' reading now could save you hours of trouble later!

Are you well connected?

If you try the electrical activities on pages 8–29, you'll find electricity only flows between things that are correctly stuck together. So when you build a circuit, make sure it has really good connections.

Ask an adult to strip the plastic off the ends of your plastic-coated wires. Electricity can only flow through the bare metal—it does not flow through plastic.

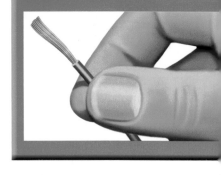

Having problems?

Don't worry if you have trouble with some of the activities in this book.

If things don't seem to be working, read through each step of the activity again and then have another try.

Remember, even the greatest scientists had problems with their experiments. Take J. J. Thompson, for example—the scientist who discovered the electron. He was so clumsy, his students would never let him go near his own equipment, but he was still a great scientist!

Stuck for words?

If you come across a word you don't understand, or you just want to find out a little more, look in the glossary on pages 30 and 31.

Warning

This book's electrical activities use small batteries that give off very little electricity.

Never experiment with electricity that comes out of plugs and sockets at home or school. It is thousands of times more powerful than a small battery. It can kill.

Attach a wire to the terminals of a battery with tape or modeling clay. Make sure the metal part of the wire touches the metal part of the battery.

Attach a wire to the terminals (ends) of your light bulb like this (left) if you have a bulb with a base, or like this (below) if you have a bulb without a base.

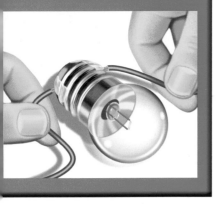

Never play near over-head pylons or electricity substations. Even when you're not touching them, electricity can jump from them and kill you.

The right stuff

To try out most of the activities in the book, you only need a few everyday things, such as batteries, spoons, lemons, and paper clips. Sometimes, you'll need items such as iron filings, steel wool, and mini light bulbs. Try your local toy or hobby shop for these.

You will also need several lengths of plastic-coated (insulated) wire.

For most of the activities, any small battery will work. Put it in a radio to make sure it isn't flat!

Small light bulbs that screw in to a base like this are the easiest type to use, or you can use bulbs without a base.

Try to get hold of two straight bar magnets.

Clock symbol

The clock symbol at the start of each experiment shows you approximately how many minutes the activity should take. All take between 5 and 30 minutes. If you are using glue, allow extra time for drying.

5

What a tingle!

Electricity is a form of energy—it makes things happen. For instance, it can heat up a toaster or a light bulb. We usually think of electricity as something that flows through wires. But there's another form of electricity that doesn't flow at all, and that is called static electricity. You can make this by rubbing certain things together, which gives one or other of them something called charge.

You will need:

- Tissue paper
- A plastic ruler
- A scrap of nylon fabric
- Scissors

Snake charmer

Use static electricity to move things with no hands! Make sure that everything you use in these activities is dry.

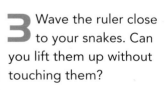

1 Copy this pattern onto the tissue paper and cut it out. Cut along the dotted line and then pull one end to make a spiraling snake. Make more snakes to go with it.

2 Rub a plastic ruler several times with a scrap of nylon fabric.

3 Wave the ruler close to your snakes. Can you lift them up without touching them?

What's going on?

When you rub the ruler, you brush tiny particles onto it. These particles, called electrons, are far too small to see, but they create static electricity. The tissue paper does not have many electrons. It moves toward the ruler so that it can grab the ones that it needs.

Fashion victim

Listen carefully while you take off some nylon or viscose clothes. If it's dark, look into a mirror while you do this. Do you hear tiny crackles? Or see tiny sparks?

You will need:

● Clothes made of nylon or viscose
● A mirror

What's going on?

The crackles that you hear and sparks that you see when you take off the clothes are caused by electrons moving between your body and the clothes. They are just like mini thunder and lightning!

Wire it up

So far, you've only experimented with static electricity made when you brush electrons on or off things. But there is another very useful type of electricity that's made by moving electrons, called current electricity. Electrons move easily through metal. Using a battery, you can push them right through a metal wire. You need to make the wire into a loop, called a circuit, that lets the electrons flow out of the battery, then in again.

You will need:

● A small flashlight bulb (with a maximum voltage of 3 or 4.5v)
● A 1.5-volt, AA battery
● Two insulated wires
● Tape

Bright idea

When a current of electricity flows through this circuit, it lights up a bulb.

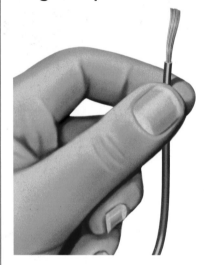

1 Ask an adult to use a sharp knife, wire cutters, or pliers to strip around ³/₄ in. (2cm) of plastic from each end of your wires.

2 Using tape, attach the bare end of one wire to the silvery knob on the top of your battery. This knob is called the positive terminal.

3 Using some more tape, attach the bare end of your other wire to the silvery base of your battery. This is called the negative terminal.

4 Connect your two free ends of wire to the light bulb. Does your bulb glow?

Bridge the gap

Follow the steps in "Bright idea" again to make your flashlight bulb glow. Ask an adult to cut one of the wires in half to break the circuit. Keep everything else in place. Now ask your adult helper to strip the two free ends of broken wire. Then, using a metal paper clip, touch both free ends of the bare wire at the same time. What happens to the bulb?

What's going on?

You have made a complete circuit. Electrons can flow out of the battery, through one wire, through the bulb, through the other wire, and into the battery again. When they flow through the bulb, they make it glow.

You will need:

- A small flashlight bulb (with a maximum voltage of 3 or 4.5v)
- A 1.5-volt, AA battery
- Two insulated wires
- A metal paper clip
- Tape

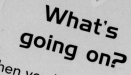

What's going on?

When you break a circuit, electricity can't flow around it, so the bulb stops glowing. The metal paper clip can bridge the gap in the broken circuit. When you press it against the two bare ends of broken wire, electricity flows through it, from one end to the other. The paper clip completes the circuit, so the bulb glows. In this way, it works as a switch.

Thick and thin

Electricity can flow through any metal wires in a circuit. But it finds it easier to flow through thick wires than through the thin ones. The amount of electricity flowing through a wire is called the current. If you use a thinner wire, a battery finds it harder to push electricity through it, so it will produce a smaller current.

What's going on?

Electricity finds it difficult to flo[w] through a circuit that contains a th[in] strand of steel wool. Your battery c[an] only make a small current in a circuit li[ke] this, so the bulb glows dimly. When yo[u] use an even thinner strand, the battery makes an even smaller current, so the bulb glows even more dimly.

Dim the light

See what happens to your bulb when you put a really thin wire in this circuit.

You will need:

- A small flashlight bulb (with a maximum voltage of 3 or 4.5v)
- 1.5-volt AA battery
- Two insulated wires
- A piece of steel wool
- Tape

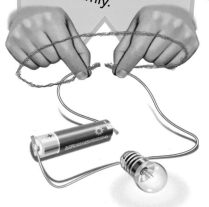

3 Use your steel wool strand, instead of a paper clip, to bridge the gap in your circuit. Check that the bulb glows.

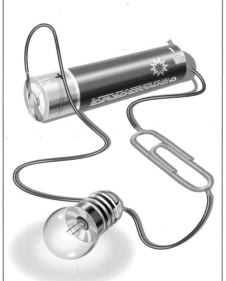

1 Follow the steps in "Bridge the gap" (page 9) to build a circuit that makes a bulb glow when you press down a paper clip.

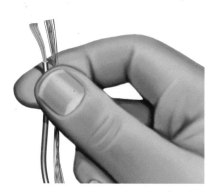

2 Pull and twist some steel wool to form a strand about 2½ in. (6cm) long. Make this strand about the same thickness as your insulated wires.

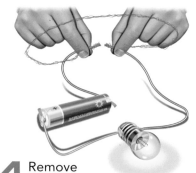

4 Remove three quarters of your steel wool to make a strand that's just as long but much thinner. Use it to bridge the gap again. How does your bulb look now?

Shortcut

The wires in this experiment could get warm, so ask an adult to help. Follow the steps in "Bright idea" (page 8) to build a circuit that makes a bulb glow. Ask an adult to strip the ends of an extra wire. Then touch the bare ends of this wire against the terminals of your battery. Make sure that you touch both terminals at the same time. What happens to the bulb?

You will need:

● A small flashlight bulb (with a maximum voltage of 3 or 4.5v)
● A 1.5-volt, AA battery
● Three insulated wires
● Tape

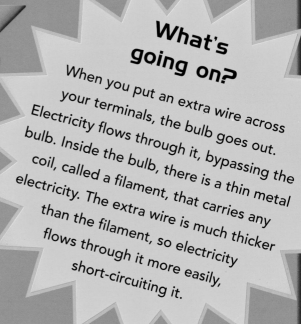

What's going on?

When you put an extra wire across your terminals, the bulb goes out. Electricity flows through it, bypassing the bulb. Inside the bulb, there is a thin metal coil, called a filament, that carries any electricity. The extra wire is much thicker than the filament, so electricity flows through it more easily, short-circuiting it.

5 Make your strand even thinner. How does this affect the bulb?

Getting warmer

Try "Dim the light" (far left) again, using only a couple of thin steel wool strands. Leave the bulb glowing dimly for a minute, then feel the steel wool. What do you notice?

What's going on?

Because electricity finds it very difficult to flow through a very thin strand of steel wool, it turns into a different form of energy—heat. This heat makes the steel wool feel slightly warmer to the touch.

11

Go with the flow

Electricity can flow through some substances more easily than through others. It can flow very easily through substances called "conductors," such as certain metals. An "insulator" is a substance that makes it practically impossible for electricity to flow. Plastics are usually good insulators.

What's going on?

The bulb glows when you put some objects, such as the metal coin, in the circuit. This is because these objects are conductors. It does not glow when you put other objects, such as the pencil eraser, in the circuit. This is because they are insulators. Conductors, unlike insulators, are made of materials that let electrons flow through them readily. This is why they let a current flow so easily.

The right stuff

Here's a handy way to tell if some everyday objects are conductors or insulators.

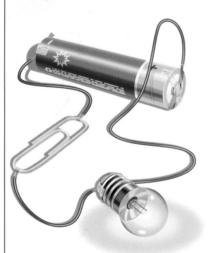

1 Follow the steps in "Bridge the gap" (page 9) to make a circuit with a break in it. Check that the bulb glows when you bridge the break with a paper clip.

2 Replace the paper clip with another object, such as a wooden spoon. Does the bulb glow? Repeat with each of your other objects. Which ones make the bulb glow and which don't?

You will need:

- A small flashlight bulb (with a maximum voltage of 3 or 4.5v)
- A 1.5-volt, AA battery
- Two insulated wires
- A metal paper clip
- Tape
- Objects made of different materials (e.g., an eraser, a coin, a drinking glass, a sheet of paper, a plastic ballpoint pen, a china teacup, a wooden spoon)

Water and air

You can test two very special substances to see whether they conduct electricity—water and air. To test water, dip your two wires into a small, water-filled bowl. To test air, simply hold your two wires up in the air.

You will need:

- A small flashlight bulb (with a maximum voltage of 3 or 4.5v)
- A 1.5-volt, AA battery
- Two insulated wires
- Tape
- A bowl of water

What's going on?

The bulb glows when you bridge the gap in your circuit with water—but not when you bridge it with air. Water, just like metal, lets electricity flow through it: it is a conductor. Air, on the other hand, is an insulator. Sometimes, electricity can flow through air—for example, when the flow of electricity is powerful. Electricity makes lightning in this way, for example.

Powerhouse

A battery is a mini electricity generator. When you put it in a circuit, it gradually releases the electrical energy stored inside it. This energy pushes a stream of electrons around the circuit, making an electric current. Believe it or not, you can actually make your own electricity generators, just like batteries, from a few coins and some supplies from the kitchen.

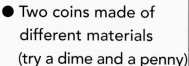

You will need:

- Two coins made of different materials (try a dime and a penny)
- A lemon
- A kitchen knife (ask an adult for this)

Fruity tingle

Make enough electricity from a lemon to feel a tingle on your tongue!

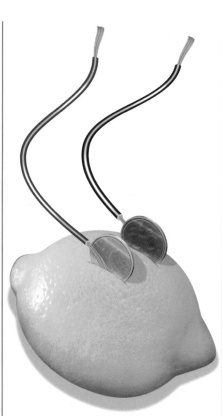

1 Ask an adult to cut two small slits in your lemon with a kitchen knife. The slits should be about 1 in. (2.5cm) apart and long enough to hold your coins.

2 Now ask your adult helper to strip about 3/4 in. (2cm) off the ends of your insulated wires. Push a bare end of one wire into each slit. Push a coin into each slit to hold the wires in place.

3 Put the loose end of each wire on your tongue, making sure that the wires don't touch. Can you feel anything?

What's going on?

Your lemon and coins make a simple battery. They can't produce enough electricity to power a light bulb, but they should make enough to feel a tingle on your tongue. If you pull out one wire, you break the circuit and don't feel the tingle any more. In a real battery, there are two plates made of different metals, just like your coins. These are separated by a type of chemical called an acid, a little like the acidic lemon juice.

Change the recipe

Lemons aren't the only fruit that will make electricity. Try "Fruity tingle" (left) again with other types of fruit and vegetables. Change your metal coins, too.

You will need:

- Coins and nails made of various materials
- Different fruit and vegetables
- Insulated wires

4 Pull one wire out of the lemon and then repeat step 3. What do you feel now?

What's going on?

Many fruit or vegetables and metals will work as mini batteries. You need an acidic food (potatoes and pineapples are good) with two metals. Some combinations produce a much bigger tingle than others.

The big push

A battery has to push electricity all the way around a circuit. If a circuit has a lot of parts that make it difficult for electricity to flow—for instance, very skinny wires—the current the battery makes will be very small. To produce more current, you need to use a battery that can give electrons a bigger push. The electrical "push" of a battery is measured in "volts" (v). A 9-volt battery, for example, has six times the push of a 1.5-volt battery.

You will need:

- A 1.5-volt, AA battery
- A 9-volt battery
- Up to five small flashlight bulbs (each with a maximum voltage of 3 or 4.5v)
- Up to six wires
- Tape

Party lights

See what happens when a battery has to push current through more than one bulb.

1 Follow the steps in "Bright idea" (page 8) to make a bulb glow. Check that the bulb is glowing and try to remember exactly how bright it looks.

2 Add another bulb to the circuit, like this. Do both bulbs glow? How bright are they?

3 Add more light bulbs to the circuit. What happens to their brightness? Do they always glow?

Dimmer switch

Follow the steps in "Bridge the gap" (page 9) to make a broken circuit. Bridge the gap in the circuit with a soft mechanical pencil lead. Does the bulb glow?

You will need:

- A 1.5-volt, AA battery
- A small light bulb
- Three wires
- Mechanical pencil lead
- Tape

What's going on?

The length of pencil lead between the wires dictates the bulb's brightness, because electricity finds it difficult to flow through lead. The longer the lead is, the less voltage there is to make the bulb glow.

What's going on?

As you put more bulbs in this circuit, each one gets dimmer. That's because the bulbs have to share the battery's voltage. The battery has to use some of its voltage to push electricity through each bulb. The current in the circuit reduces every time a bulb is added. If a lot are added, the current becomes so low that it can't make the bulbs glow at all. A 9-volt battery pushes more current around the circuit, so it can make more bulbs glow.

4 While you have three or more bulbs in the circuit, swap your battery for a 9-volt one and see what happens.

Feel the force

All magnets can do two things: they can pull iron or nickel objects toward them, and they can attract or repel other magnets. Some magnets occur naturally. They have special magnetic properties as soon as they are mined. Others are made from nonmagnets, often using electricity. Materials that are attracted toward magnets, such as iron or nickel, are called "magnetic materials."

You will need:
● A magnet
● Steel pins

What's going on?

Steel pins stick to a magnet becau... steel contains a lot of iron. The mag... pulls the most strongly at its ends, so m... the pins will stick there. Scientists call t... ends of the magnet its "poles." When a ... sticks to the magnet, it becomes part of it, so it can pick up more pins itself. That's why you can pick up a chain of pins.

Jump to it!

Next time someone drops some pins, help them pick them up with a magnet!

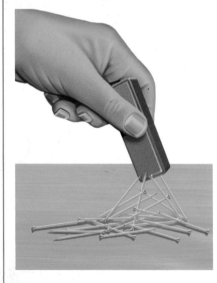

1 Bring your magnet close to a small pile of loose pins. Can you pick up the pins with your magnet?

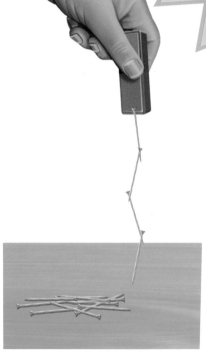

2 Try to pick up a chain of pins with the magnet. How many pins can you pick up in this way?

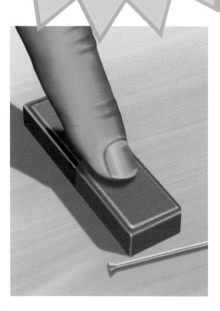

3 Put one pin on the table and then gradually move the magnet closer to it. What happens?

Is it magnetic?

Find out which materials are magnetic by picking up objects around your home. (Warning! Magnets damage TVs and computers, so stay away from these!) Only objects with iron or nickel in them are attracted to the magnet. You may have found these materials in coins or keys. The magnet has no effect on objects such as the spoon and eraser because these don't contain iron or nickel. For the same reason, it has no effect on the foil—it's made of aluminum.

You will need:

- A magnet
- Objects made of different materials (e.g., wooden spoon, metal paper clips, aluminum foil, plastic pen top, pencil eraser, key, coins, stone, soda can, puddle of water)

Can sorter

You can use a magnet to sort steel and aluminum cans for recycling. Using the string and tape, dangle your magnet from the bottom of a chair so that it is about 4 in. (10cm) above the ground. Roll your cans under the magnet, one at a time. Do all the cans roll past the magnet smoothly?

You will need:

- Empty food and soda cans
- A magnet
- String
- A wooden chair
- Tape

What's going on?

The aluminum cans roll past the magnet, but the steel cans slow down. They may even stop or stick to the magnet, because steel is a magnetic material. At recycling centers, cans are often sorted by moving them along a conveyor belt past a line of magnets.

19

Pole to pole

Every magnet has two distinct poles. We call them "north" and "south" poles (see page 26). The area of force around a magnet is called its "magnetic field." Try using magnets to create funny effects!

Opposites attract

The forces between the two poles can be strong—strong enough for you to feel them.

You will need: 🕐

● A ruler
● A pencil
● Two bar magnets

1 Take a close look at your two bar magnets. There should be paint marks on their ends to tell you which pole is which. They may be labeled "north" or "south," or they may simply be painted different colors.

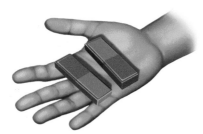

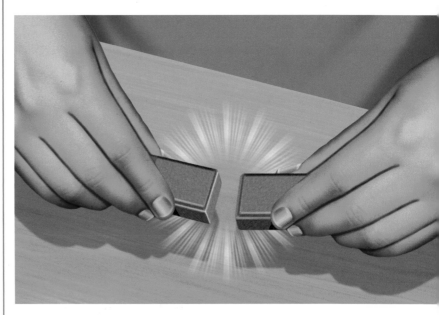

2 Bring two opposite poles of your two magnets close to each other. Can you feel the force that pulls them together?

3 Turn one of your magnets around so that two like poles are facing each other. What force can you feel now?

Hold the magnets 1 in. (3cm) apart, then 2 in. (6cm), etc. How close do the magnets have to be to make a force you can feel?

Spider stealth

Draw a spider about 2 in. (5cm) across and cut it out. Tape a paper clip to the bottom of your spider and put it onto the sheet of cardboard. You can make it move wherever you want using a magnet hidden underneath the cardboard! Anyone watching will see the spider move around in a mysterious way!

You will need:

- Paper and scissors
- A large sheet of thin cardboard
- Felt-tip pens
- A steel paper clip
- Tape
- A small magnet

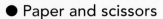

What's going on?

If your magnet is strong enough, the force between the paper clip and the magnet will make the spider move around, even though it's separated from the magnet by the cardboard.

Dancing socks

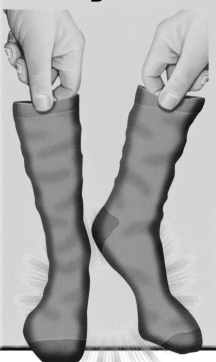

Put a magnet inside each sock and dangle the socks in the air. Move the socks close together and watch them dance around! Pad the socks out by wrapping each magnet in a couple of layers of paper. Does the trick still work? Now put several more layers of paper around the magnets.

You will need:

- Two bar magnets
- A pair of socks
- Paper

What's going on?

Unless your magnets are weak, they will attract or repel each other, even if covered by socks. A little paper won't change this, but many layers will. The stronger the magnets, the more paper you can wrap around them before the dancing stops.

21

Magnetic art

Magnets aren't only useful for making machines and tools. With a little imagination, you can also use them to create magnetic works of art! You can make interesting moving sculptures, like the one below, or fascinating pictures of a magnet's forces.

Freaky pendulum

Three magnets will make this sculpture that swings in the strangest of ways.

You will need:

- Three magnets
- An iron nail
- String
- A chair
- Modeling clay
- Tape

1 Tie some string to the head of your nail. Then dangle the nail from under the chair. Make sure that one of your magnets can fit under the nail, with a gap of about 1/3 in. (1cm).

2 Tap the nail gently and watch it swing back and forth like a pendulum. Make sure that there are no magnets near your nail when you do this.

3 Using modeling clay, attach three magnets to the floor. Make sure the same poles face each other. They should be 3/4 in. (2cm) apart.

What's going on?

Most filings settle around the poles because the force of the magnet is the greatest here. Others settle in onion-shaped rings around the magnet. These rings are called "lines of force." The pattern of the filings is symmetrical because the magnet creates exactly the same force at each pole and on each side.

You will need:

- A bar magnet
- Iron filings
- Paint
- An old toothbrush
- A blank piece of paper

Get the picture

Place your magnet under a piece of paper. Sprinkle iron filings on the paper. They will form a definite pattern because the magnet is under the paper. Put a little paint on your toothbrush, then flick the toothbrush with your finger to spray paint onto the paper. When the paint is dry, carefully remove the magnet and filings.

4 Move the chair so that the nail is directly over the center of the magnets. Then gently tap the nail again. What happens next?

What's going on?

When there are no magnets around, the nail swings back and forth smoothly, just like a pendulum. The only force the nail feels is gravity. When the magnets are beneath the nail, it swings crazily, because it also feels a force from each magnet. As it swings nearer and farther from each magnet, the force on it varies continually.

Make your own magnets

Every magnet is made up of billions of tiny magnets, called "domains," that are all lined up in the same direction. Other materials have domains, too, but theirs are all jumbled up. If you have a magnet, you can tease the domains of magnetic materials to make them face the same way. In this way, you can make more magnets of your own.

At a stroke

To turn a paper clip into a magnet, you just have to stroke it the right way.

You will need:

- Two steel paper clips
- Modeling clay
- A magnet

1 Untwist a steel paper clip and lay it on a firm surface. Hold it in place with some modeling clay.

What's going on?

When you stroke a steel paper clip with a magnet, you turn the paper clip into a magnet, too. This is because the magnet pulls at the domains of the paper clip until they all face in one direction. The magnet can move the domains around because the domains themselves are microscopic magnets.

2 Holding your bar magnet in one hand, move it through the air in a loop like this, close to the paper clip. Repeat this several times. Make sure to keep your magnet facing the same way. Never change the direction of the loop.

Magnetic mobile

Make a magnetic mobile and see how long it lasts. Follow the steps in "At a stroke" (left) to magnetize lots of things. Suspend your largest object from a piece of string just above floor level and then link together as many of the other objects as you can. Be careful when using nails in this experiment. Keep the items together using the magnetic forces between them—don't use tape or glue. Check your mobile to see what happens.

You will need:

- A magnet
- String and a selection of lightweight iron and steel objects (e.g., steel paper clips, an iron nail, and a steel key)

3 Move your magnet out of the way, pick up your steel paper clip, and test it. Is it a magnet? Can you pick up another paper clip with it?

What's going on?

As each part of this mobile is a magnet, it holds in place without glue, although the force will reduce over time. Steel objects stay magnetic longer than iron ones because their domains are harder to jumble.

Map it out

Ever since people discovered magnets, they have used them to find their way from place to place. Magnets can be used to navigate because they always turn around to face roughly north. This is because they are affected by Earth, which itself acts like a very big but weak magnet. A magnet used to find north is called a compass.

Traveling light

This compass, which can fit in a matchbox, is also light enough to float on water.

1 Follow the instructions in "At a stroke" (page 24) to turn a steel pin into a magnet. Use your magnet to do this.

You will need:

- A magnet
- A steel pin
- A bottle cork
- Modeling clay
- A large plastic bowl
- Water
- A knife (ask an adult)
- A piece of paper

2 Ask an adult to cut a small disk, about 1/2 in. (1cm) thick, from the end of your cork with a knife. Place the pin on top of the cork. Hold it in place with a tiny amount of modeling clay.

3 Fill the bowl with water and then carefully float the steel pin and cork in it.

What's going on?

The magnetized steel pin always lies in the same direction, roughly north–south, even if you turn the bowl. It does this because its north and south poles are attracted by Earth. One of Earth's magnetic poles is roughly north on the map; the other is roughly south.

Turn around

You can confuse your compass with a magnet. Follow the steps in "Traveling light" (left) to make a floating mini compass. Check that it points in a north–south direction when it settles. Then bring a magnet a couple of inches away from your compass. What happens?

You will need:

- A magnet
- The same items used in "Traveling light"

4 Wait for the steel pin and cork to stop turning. Draw a picture of the pin on a piece of paper. Lie it on the floor and note which way the needle faces.

What's going on?

When a magnet is close to your compass, the compass poles spin toward the magnet's poles, so the compass stops pointing north. That's because your magnet is much stronger than Earth's magnetic effect.

27

Pick-up power

Electricity and magnetism are very closely connected. When electricity flows through a wire, it turns the wire into a magnet. Coiled wire concentrates this magnetism so that it is strong enough to pick up things. When you move a magnet near a wire, you make a tiny current. Our homes are full of machines that use the connection between electricity and magnetism. We call this link "electromagnetism."

What's going on?

When the switch is in place, the iron nail picks up pins because electricity flows through the circuit, turning its wires into magnets. The coil wire concentrates this magnetism, so the force is strong enough to turn the nail into a magnet. A magnet like this, which only works when electricity flows around it, is called an "electromagnet."

Electric magnet

Send electricity through a coil of wire to make a strong magnet. The wire could get warm—ask an adult for help.

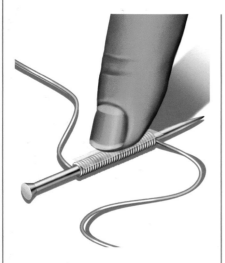

1 Wind the wire tightly around the iron nail at least ten times, holding it in place with tape.

2 Connect the wire to the nail to a terminal of your 9-volt battery. Connect the other end to the other terminal and add a paper clip switch (see page 9).

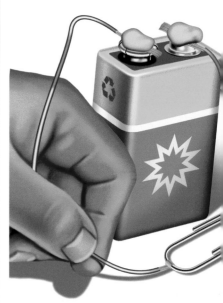

3 Hold the nail over a pile of steel pins. What happens? Remove the paper clip switch to turn off the circuit. What happens now?

You will need:

- An iron nail
- A very long wire with plastic coating
- A paper clip
- A 9-volt battery
- Tape
- Steel pins

Electric eels

Follow the steps in "Electric magnet" (left) to make an electromagnet. Then challenge a friend to a game of "electric eels." Cut out some eels from tissue paper and then stick a little steel wool to their heads. Take turns to pick up eels, against the clock, using only your electromagnet. Turning it on and off at the right time is crucial. If you pick up one eel, you can keep it, but if you pick up more than one, you must throw them back!

You will need:

- The electromagnet made in "Electric magnet" (opposite)
- Tissue paper
- Steel wool
- Tape

What's going on?

As the eels have steel wool heads, you can pick them up with your electromagnet. The nail is only magnetized when the paper clip switch is on. When it is off, there is no current, and therefore no magnetism.

Glossary

ATTRACT Two things attract each other if they want to pull themselves closer together. This happens when they have opposite electrical charges (when one has too many electrons, and the other has too few). A magnet will attract objects that contain a lot of iron or nickel. Two magnets will attract each other if the north pole of one is close to the south pole of the other.

CHARGE Something has charge if it has too many or too few electrons. This could happen because you've rubbed it with another object to make static electricity. Two objects have the same type of charge if they've both lost electrons or both gained them. They have "opposite" charges if one has gained electrons but the other has lost them.

COMPASS A device that can be used to find out roughly where north is. The most important part of a compass is the pointer, which is a magnet. Like all magnets, the pointer will end up lying in a roughly north–south direction when it is left to swing freely.

CONDUCTOR A substance that electricity can flow through easily. Metal and water are both good conductors. Metal is the raw material of many electrical devices—for instance, wires, switches, and light bulbs. Copper and silver are both good conductors, but silver is too expensive to be used often. You may also come across the word "conductor" when people are talking about things other than electricity. For instance, engineers often ask if a material is a good conductor of heat.

CURRENT A measure of how much electricity is flowing. Current is measured in amps (A). A circuit will have a bigger current if a battery finds it easier to push electricity around it. A larger current means that more electrons are flowing through the circuit.

DOMAINS The millions of mini magnets, much too tiny to see, that make up every material. The domains of a magnet all face in the same direction. Their magnetism will reduce if the domains get jumbled—for instance, because they have been bashed with a hammer.

ELECTRICITY The form of energy that makes toasters, lights, televisions, and all other electrical things work. Electricity is created by particles, called electrons, that are much too tiny to see. Electrons make "current electricity" when they flow through things such as wires or light bulbs. When they are not moving, electrons make "static electricity."

ELECTROMAGNET A magnet that only works when electricity flows through it. Most electromagnets are made of a coil of wire, which is wrapped around some metal. The wire coil will boost the metal's magnetic strength.

ELECTRON A tiny particle that is much too small to see. There are one or more electrons in every atom. When electrons flow through things—for instance, a wire—they make current electricity. When they rub off one thing and onto another, they make static electricity.

FILAMENT The thin, coiled wire inside a light bulb that makes the bulb glow. Electricity finds it difficult to flow through this wire, so it turns into another form of energy—heat. This makes the filament glow white-hot, producing light.

INSULATOR A substance that makes it very difficult for electricity to flow. Wood, paper, glass, and plastic are all good insulators. Electric machines and parts are often covered in insulators to make them safe—for instance, wires are often covered in plastic, and a television is built inside a plastic box. People also use the word "insulator" when they're not talking about electricity. For instance, they might look for a material that's a good insulator of heat.

MAGNET An object that can pull iron or nickel objects toward it. Magnets can also attract or repel other magnets. Some rocks, like magnetite, are naturally occurring magnets. Other magnets can be made in the laboratory—for instance, by stroking iron or nickel with other magnets.

MAGNETIC FIELD The area around a magnet where it can noticeably attract or repel things. Stronger magnets have a larger magnetic field.

MAGNETIC MATERIALS Materials that are attracted toward magnets. Iron and nickel are magnetic materials. So are many materials that contain either of these two metals. Steel, for instance, contains a lot of iron so it is a magnetic material.

PARALLEL The word used to describe electrical parts that have been wired into two or more separate loops. Each loop lets electricity flow out of the battery, through itself, and then back into the battery again.

POLES The two areas of a magnet, usually at its ends, where the magnet's pull is the strongest. If you let a magnet swing freely, one pole will always end up pointing approximately south. This is the magnet's "south pole." The other, the "north pole," will point roughly north. The poles end up pointing in these directions because they are attracted to the north and south poles of Earth, which is itself a giant magnet.

REPEL Two things repel each other if they want to push themselves farther apart. This happens when they have the same type of electrical charge (when both objects have too few electrons or both have too many). Two magnets will repel each other if the north pole of one is close to the north pole of another; they also repel if their south poles are close together.

SERIES The word used to describe electrical things that have been strung together in a single loop. This loop lets electricity flow out of the battery, through each part, then into the battery again.

SHORT-CIRCUIT A very easy path that electricity can take around a circuit. A wire directly connected to the two terminals of a battery will make a short-circuit. Electricity will always take a short-circuit when it can.

STATIC ELECTRICITY
A type of electricity that you can make by rubbing certain things together—for instance, a nylon cloth and a plastic ruler. When you do this, you brush electrons off one item and onto another. This gives both objects an electrical "charge."

VOLTAGE A measure of the electrical "push" that a battery can give to the electrons flowing around a circuit. This push is measured in volts (v). Most batteries have their voltage printed on their casing.

Websites

If you have enjoyed this book, the websites below will give you even more information on electricity and magnets. Many of them have fun games to play that will help you to understand the difficult information.

Electricity:
● www.switchedonkids.org.uk
● www.bbc.co.uk/schools/ks2bitesize/science/physical_processes
● www.engineeringinteract.org/resources/siliconspies/siliconspieslink.htm
● www.andythelwell.com/blobz/guide.html

Magnets:
● www.primaryonline.co.uk/sitetour/pol/magnet.html
● www.bbc.co.uk/schools/ks2bitesize/science/physical_processes/magnet_springs/read1.shtml
● www.engineeringinteract.org/resources/parkworldplot/flash/concepts/magneticforces.htm

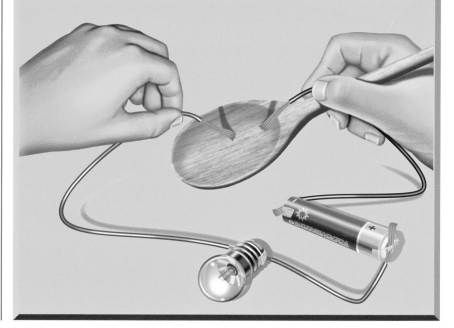

8,9   14,15

Index

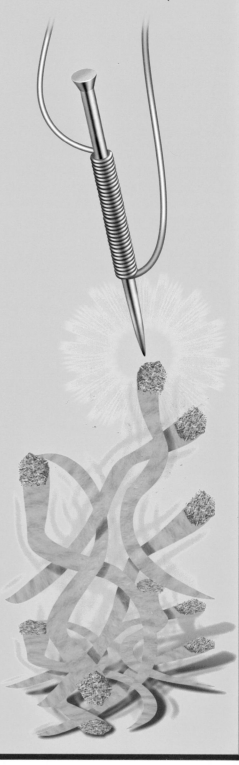